BE

By Amire Ben Salmi

Your

The Ultimate Guide to Unlocking Your Full Potential

Brand

It's time to learn how to Dream Big without limits! - the question is are you ready to soar to new heights?...

BE YOUR BRAND
-
THE ULTIMATE GUIDE TO UNLOCKING YOUR FULL POTENTIAL

Published by I AM Publishing House

Interior and cover design by Lashai Ben Salmi

Paperback ISBN: 978-1-915862-32-7
Hardback ISBN: 978-1-915862-31-0

BE YOUR BRAND

YOUR PERSONAL BRAND
IS YOUR SUPER POWER

BE

By Amire Ben Salmi

Your

The Ultimate Guide to Unlocking Your Full Potential

Brand

It's time to learn how to Dream Big without limits! - the question is are you ready to soar to new heights?...

DEDICATION

DEDICATION

This book is dedicated to every young dreamer who dares to believe in the power of their voice.

To my incredible family, your love, support and encouragement have been the foundation of my journey. You inspire me every day to keep pushing forward and striving for greatness.

To my mentors and teachers. Thank you for guiding me with wisdom and kindness. Your belief in me has shaped the person **I AM** becoming.

And to every child who has ever been told their dreams are too big. This book is for you. May you always know that your words matter, your stories deserve to be told, and your potential is limitless.

Keep dreaming, keep writing, and never stop believing in yourself.

With love and gratitude,

Amire Ben Salmi

ACKNOWLEDGEMENTS

ACKNOWLEDGEMENTS

I want to express my deepest gratitude to everyone who has supported and inspired me throughout this journey. Writing this book has been a labour of love, and I could not have done it alone.

A heartfelt thank you to my family for their unwavering encouragement, patience, and belief in my vision. Your love and support have been my foundation. To my mentors and teachers, thank you for guiding me with wisdom and kindness, and helping me grow not just as a writer but as a person.

I also want to acknowledge the incredible impact of small yet meaningful acts of kindness. Whether it's a simple smile, a thoughtful message, or a helping hand, kindness has the power to transform lives. To those who have shown me generosity and compassion, your actions have left a lasting imprint on my heart.

To my readers, thank you for taking this journey with me. May this book inspire you to embrace kindness, uplift others, and believe in the power of your own story. Lastly, to every dreamer and aspiring author out there. Never let anyone tell you it's too late or too early to pursue your dreams. Keep writing, keep believing, and most importantly, keep spreading kindness.

With gratitude,

Amire Ben Salmi

CONTENTS

CONTENTS

INTRODUCTION

INTRODUCTION

Hey Trailblazer,

*You are not reading this book by accident. In fact, I do not believe in coincidences - only God-incidences. Therefore, **YOU** are reading this book because there's something very special inside **YOU**... a spark, a message, a solution, , an invention, an idea, a song, a dream, a vibe etc that is meant to shine.*

*Maybe **YOU** don't know what it is just yet, and that's totally okay. This book is **Your** map. **Your** megaphone. **Your** mirror. **Your** launchpad.*

*"**Be Your Brand - The Ultimate Guide to Unlocking Your Full Potential**" isn't just a book.*

*It's a movement and **YOU** are the leader. So, what does "**being your brand**" even mean?*

*It means showing up in the world as **YOU** boldly, authentically, kindly, lovingly, compassionately, empathically, honestly and consistently because **YOU ARE ENOUGH...** just the way **YOU** are. Not who someone else expects **YOU** to be. Not a watered-down version of **YOUR TRUE SELF**. But, the full bright and brilliant **YOU**.*

*When **YOU** live with clarity, confidence and character, **YOU** do not follow trends, **YOU** set them. When **YOU** choose commitment, creativity and courage, **YOU** don't wait for permission to **BE YOU. YOU** simply step into your power.*

***YOU** can build your own stage. When **YOU** communicate and collaborate, **YOU** give birth to possibility and make a real impact to make the world a better place for everyone.*

*This book was written with **YOU** in mind, for your inner child, the young visionary in **YOU**, the quiet dreamer, the loud thinker, the future founder, the everyday **CHANGE-MAKER**.*

INTRODUCTION

Inside this book you'll learn how to:

- *Find **YOUR** voice*
- *Follow **YOUR** dreams*
- *Build **YOUR** skills*
- *Create **YOUR** future*

*And in the final bonus chapter, you'll discover the secret most people don't learn until they're **25**, **35**, **55** or maybe **NEVER**... and that is called **Positioning**. It's how **YOU** take your gifts and get noticed, respected and taken seriously.*

*This book has the potential to totally transform your mindset and life forever, but only if **YOU ARE WILLING** to do the inner work and take massive action.*

By the end of this book, you won't just feel inspired. You'll be equipped to act.

Because your brand is not just a logo.
*It is about the promises that you make and the promises that you keep, while becoming the best version of **YOU**.*
It's your legacy.

Let's build it together.

*Are **YOU**, ready? **C'mon - let's go**.*

Amire Ben Salmi

BE

By Amire Ben Salmi

Your

The Ultimate Guide to Unlocking Your Full Potential

Brand

It's time to learn how to Dream Big without limits! - the question is are you ready to soar to new heights?...

Chapter *One*

Clarity – Know What You Want

CHAPTER 1

Chapter 1*, *Clarity – Know What You Want, sets the foundation for everything that follows in this journey of personal growth. It introduces the idea that life can feel overwhelming, for example you could be gazing at 100 ice cream flavours, but if we don't take time to focus. Without clarity, it's easy to get stuck in a loop of indecision, wasting time and energy without real progress. This chapter helps you understand that clarity isn't about choosing forever, but choosing for now... in the moment. When you as a young trailblazer pick one area to explore deeply, you can begin building momentum and confidence in yourself.

Below is a story about Jayden, who is a kid who loves soccer, coding, and drawing... you will see how scattered energy can lead to feeling confused or unproductive. But one wise nudge from his teacher unlocked everything: just choose one thing for now. Jayden's choice to focus on coding for 3 months allowed him to create something real... a game! This small shift in mindset teaches a powerful truth: clarity leads to action, and action builds results. It's not about ignoring your passions, it's about committing to one, long enough to grow.

This chapter also introduces an empowering tool: asking deep, reflective questions across six categories: Who, What, When, Where, Why, and How.

These questions have been created to help you break down any goal, challenge, or idea with clarity and strategic thinking. Along with a practical activity... writing down three passions, picking one, and helping you to set a small goal. You will be gently guided into turning your curiosity into commitment. Clarity is the compass that turns your big dreams into simple steps. Once you know what you want, everything else starts to line up.

Imagine going to an ice cream shop with 100 flavours to choose from, but you just stare at the wall. That's what life feels like without clarity. You can often feel stuck, confused and wasting time despite all the options that are set out in front of you.

Story Time:

Jayden loved soccer, coding and drawing. But, he kept jumping from one thing to the next. Then one day, his teacher said, "You don't have to choose forever, but you do have to choose for now."

Boom!...

Jayden focused on coding for 3 months and built his first gaming app!

Try This:

- Write 3 things you love doing
- Circle ONE of those things that you want to focus on for the next 30 days
- Set a small goal (for example: “speak to 5-10 new people in your area of interest, develop your personal brand, write a page a day for a new book, practice coding, post a solution on social media each day, practice public speaking etc”)

Take a moment to reflect on the following questions:

I want you to take a moment to go through each of the questions below and answer them in conjunction to the idea and/or solution to a problem that you wish to focus on.

Who

1. Who is affected by this issue?
2. Who faces the biggest consequences?
3. Who holds the power in this situation?
4. Who might see this differently?
5. Who are the key stakeholders involved?
6. Who benefits from this outcome?
7. Who else should be consulted?
8. Who can provide more information?

What

1. What is the issue at hand?
2. What are the main arguments?
3. What is the evidence?
4. What assumptions are being made?
5. What are the potential consequences?
6. What alternatives exist?
7. What are the risks of each alternative?
8. What steps can be taken next?

When

1. When did this issue first emerge?
2. When do the effects typically appear?
3. When was the data last collected?
4. When is the best time to act?
5. When have solutions been attempted?
6. When is the deadline for action?
7. When should you expect to see results?
8. When will you review progress?

Where

1. Where did this first become an issue?
2. Where is the problem most evident?
3. Where can you find supporting data?
4. Where have solutions worked before?
5. Where are resources most needed?
6. Where are potential obstacles located?
7. Where can you implement solutions first?
8. Where should you monitor the outcomes?

Why

1. Why is this issue significant?
2. Why did it arise in the first place?
3. Why are certain solutions preferred?
4. Why might opinions differ?
5. Why has this not been addressed sooner?
6. Why are some more affected than others?
7. Why is immediate action necessary?
8. Why should you revisit it in the future?

How

1. How did this issue start?
2. How does this impact different groups?
3. How can you gather more data?
4. How have others tackled similar issues?
5. How will you implement the solution?
6. How will you measure success?
7. How should you communicate changes?
8. How often should you reassess?

Excellent job, well done for powering through all of the above questions. I hope that they helped to give you more clarity on your desired topic of interest and be sure to do some research online.

Chapter *Two*

Confidence - Believe in Yourself

CHAPTER 2

Chapter 2, Confidence – Believe in Yourself, is a powerful reminder that you don't need to be perfect to take action, you just need to believe that you can grow. Confidence isn't loud or flashy. It's the quiet decision to show up, try again, and trust that your future self is stronger than your current fear. This chapter aims to help you see that confidence is not something that you are born with, but as something you consciously build, through repetition, courage, and self-belief.

Maya's story below will bring this chapter to life. In this story, she was always picked last in gym class, which made her feel invisible and unimportant. But instead of giving up, she made a bold choice: to practice in private and surprise everyone later. after two months of quiet effort led to a huge moment, she scored the winning goal, and the crowd erupted.

This story will show that confidence isn't about waiting for others to believe in you, it's about believing in yourself first and then letting your actions speak.

This chapter offers a "Power Practice" to strengthen your inner voice: a daily routine of saying three simple but powerful affirmations. These help you as a young trailblazer to replace doubt with determination and celebrate effort over perfection. There's also a fun creative challenge to draw yourself as "Captain Confidence" a superhero version of you who keeps going no matter what. By blending mindset work, storytelling, and creativity, this chapter teaches you that confidence grows every time you choose courage over comfort.

After all, confidence isn't about being the best. It's about showing up, even when you're not sure. It's trusting your future self.

Story Time:
Maya got picked last in gym every time. But she told herself: "I'm gonna practice until I shock them." so she practice daily and then two months later, she scored the winning goal. The crowd went wild.

The Power Practice:

Say these every morning:

- "I can figure things out."
- "Mistakes mean I'm learning."
- "I am proud of trying."

Activity:

I want you to set some time aside to write down how you will practice daily. Then close your eyes and visualise seeing yourself getting better and better every day.

Chapter Three

Commitment – Stick With It (Even When It's Boring)

CHAPTER 3

Chapter 3, Commitment – Stick With It (Even When It's Boring), is all about the power of perseverance and pushing through when the excitement fades. We all hit moments where things feel "meh" or dull. When the initial thrill of starting something new wears off, and we're left with the real work.

CHAPTER 3

That's when commitment becomes essential. Champions aren't always the ones who get things right the first time; they're the ones who keep showing up, even when it's tough, and even when no one is watching. This chapter will help you to realise that success is not about avoiding the boring parts... it's about embracing them.

The story below is based on Mohamed and his podcast perfectly illustrates this point. Mohamed and his friend started their podcast with excitement, but after just three episodes, they had only two listeners... one of whom was their grandma. Instead of giving up, Mohamed decided to stick with it until they hit 10 listeners. By episode eight, their audience had grown to 500. This story highlights how progress is often slower than we expect, and how consistency, rather than immediate results, is the key to success. Mohamed's commitment to keep going, even when it didn't seem to be "working," led to a breakthrough. It's a reminder that the magic often happens just beyond the moment when we feel like quitting.

The chapter wraps up with a practical Commitment Challenge to help you build your own consistency. By choosing one goal and sticking with it for at least 21 days, you will begin to understand the importance of daily effort. Using a "Goal Tracker" could help you to stay accountable and you will be able to visually see your progress. The challenge emphasises that commitment isn't about avoiding the hard or boring moments, it's about staying in the game long enough to reach the finish line. By embracing the process, even when it feels slow, you will begin to realise that success is built, step by step, through commitment.

There's always a "meh" moment in any journey. Champions simply push through it.

Story Time:

Mohamed started a podcast with his friends. After 3 episodes, they had 2 listeners... one was his grandma. They all felt like giving up. At times they were made fun of because they did not have many followers. Mohamed had a moment when he had to dig deep down inside of himself and then he said, "Let's keep going until we hit 100." all his friends agreed and by episode 50, they had 500, by episode 100 they hit a whopping 10K followers which totally blew their minds and they were all glad that they did not give up.

Challenge:
Pick one goal. Stick with it for at least 21 days. You could use a "Goal Tracker" to keep track of each day you show up.

Chapter *Four*

Consistency – Practice Makes Room for Improvement

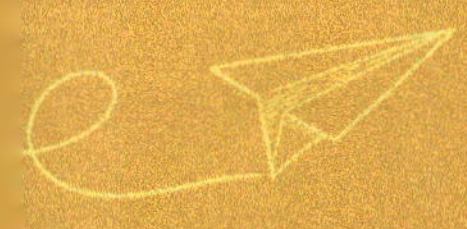

CHAPTER 4

Chapter 4, Consistency – Practice Makes Room for Improvement, this chapter emphasises that true greatness doesn't come from a single big achievement, but from small, steady actions repeated over time. It's easy to admire someone's success without seeing the daily effort behind it. Consistency may not seem exciting in the moment, but it builds real momentum and lasting results. The idea is simple: doing a little every day is far more powerful than doing a lot once in a while.

The story below is based on Zara, it aims to perfectly illustrates this. She didn't start off as a star violinist, she simply committed to practicing for just 15 minutes every morning. No big leaps, just daily discipline. After a year of consistent effort, she confidently performed on stage. People praised her talent, but what they were really seeing was the result of her quiet, regular practice. Her story is a reminder that showing up every day, even in small ways, can lead to impressive transformation.

To help build this kind of consistency in your own life, try the “Daily Power Plan.” Each day, commit to: 1 thing to learn, 1 thing to create, and 1 thing to do for someone else. These three small actions keep your mind growing, your creativity flowing, and your heart connected to others. Over time, these daily wins compound and that’s how ‘Practice Makes Room for Improvement’ truly begins.

Always remember that greatness isn’t about big wins once. It’s about little wins over and over again.

Story Time:
Zara played the violin every morning for just 15 minutes. Some mornings Zara did not feel like practising, but after a moment of silence she heard an inner voice say "You can do it, keep going. You are almost there.". One year later, she played on stage. People said "Wow, you're so talented!" but really, it was just consistency.

Challenge:

Create a "Daily Power Plan":

- 1 thing to learn
- 1 thing to create
- 1 thing to do for someone else

Chapter Five

Courage – Do the Scary Thing Anyway

CHAPTER 5

Chapter 5 is all about courage - not the absence of fear, but the decision to move forward in spite of it. Fear is a natural feeling when we're stepping outside of our comfort zone, but courage kicks in when we take action anyway. Whether it's speaking up, trying something new, or facing a challenge, real bravery is found in doing the hard thing even when your heart is racing.

The story below is based on Diego, it shows how courage can look in everyday life. Diego was terrified of presenting in front of his peers. Instead of avoiding it, he practiced quietly each night, in front of his mirror. On presentation day, his hands shook and his voice trembled, but he stood up and delivered his talk. The applause he received wasn't just for his words, it was for his bravery. His courage inspired others, even if it didn't feel perfect in the moment.

To build your own courage, try the Power Move challenge: do one thing this week that makes your stomach flip a little. Maybe it's speaking in front of a group, asking a bold question, or joining something new. These small brave steps stretch your confidence and remind you that you're stronger than your fear.

Courage doesn't mean you're not afraid - it means you feel the fear and do it anyway.

Story Time:
Diego was afraid to present to his peers. He practiced in front of mirror every night. On the big day, his voice shook, but he did it. His clapped like crazy, then stood up to give him a standing-ovation.

Power Move:
Do 1 thing this week that makes your stomach flip a little. Speak, stand up, ask a question, join a new club.

Chapter *Six*

Creativity – Let Your Imagination Run Wild

CHAPTER 6

Chapter 6 celebrates creativity - the unique spark inside you that turns ordinary ideas into something magical. Creativity isn't just about art or music; it's about thinking in new ways, solving problems, and expressing yourself freely. It's your secret sauce, the thing that makes your voice, your vision, and your ideas stand out in the world.

The story below is based on Amira, for example. She didn't need fancy tools or a big budget. She grabbed some old socks, turned them into puppets, and created a fun story. When she posted her video on YouTube, she didn't expect much, but by the next week, it had over 1,000 views! Her imagination turned forgotten socks into characters and her room into a stage. That's the power of creativity: it opens doors you didn't even know were there.

Now it's your turn. Try this simple challenge: Create a character, write their story, and imagine the world they live in. Don't worry if it's silly or strange... that's the fun part. Let your imagination run wild, and remember: ***the moment you create something, no matter how small, you are a creator.***

Creativity is your secret sauce. It's how you turn ideas into magic and render the world pleasantly speechless.

Story Time:

Amira turned her old socks into puppets. Initially her family and friends did not approve and said no one would be interested in her strange and wired idea. Amira, simply said to herself "I give myself permission to let my imagination run FREE", it was at that moment that Amira tapped into her imagination and set herself free. She made up a story and posted it on YouTube. The next week.. she had over 1,000 views. Creativity opens doors.

Create This:

- Create a character
- Write their story
- Draw their world
- Boom! You're a creator.

Chapter Seven

Communication – Speak Up, Listen Up

CHAPTER 7

Chapter 7 is all about communication - the power of words to express who you are, connect with others, and make an impact. Being able to speak clearly and listening carefully are superpowers that help you shine in school, friendships, work, university, and life. Whether you're giving a speech, having a conversation, or just sharing your thoughts, how you use your voice matters.

Jules once struggled with this. He used to mumble through presentations, nervous and unsure. But instead of giving up, he started practicing in front of the mirror, one small step at a time.

By the time the school talent show came around, Jules stood tall and spoke with confidence and the audience loved it. His journey shows that communication is a skill you can build with practice and patience.

To boost your own communication skills, try these Mini Missions: compliment three people this week, ask one deep or meaningful question, and say what you really feel with kindness. These small actions can build trust, spark connection, and help your voice grow stronger every day.

Words are power. When you learn how to use them... you shine.

Story Time:
Jules used to mumble during presentations. Then he started practicing speeches in front of the mirror. By the school talent show? He crushed it.

Mini Missions:

- Compliment 3 people this week
- Ask one deep question
- Say what you really feel (with kindness)

Chapter Eight

Collaboration – Teamwork Makes the Dream Work

CHAPTER 8

Chapter 8 focuses on collaboration - the power of working together to achieve something bigger than you could on your own. Sure, doing things alone can work, but when people combine their strengths, energy, and ideas, amazing things happen. Collaboration isn't just about sharing tasks... it's about sharing vision, effort, and success.

Leila's story below shows this beautifully. She had a dream to create a community garden, but she knew she couldn't do it alone. So she reached out to her neighbours and invited them to help. By the end of spring, 14 families were growing food side by side, sharing laughs, stories, and fresh vegetables. What started as her idea became a shared project and something far more powerful than she imagined.

Your mission? Team up. Join a group, start something new with a friend, or help build someone else's idea. Whether it's a project, a club, or just a fun plan, collaboration turns "me" into "we." And that's where the real magic begins.

Did you know?... that you can either watch the movie, be in the movie, direct the movie or produce the movie... the question is, which one are you currently doing and what will you choose to do next?

More importantly learn to cherish, respect and appreciate those who come into your life as destiny helpers to help you build your dreams and aspirations. After all, people will be in our lives for a reason, a season or a life time so treat them well while they walk the journey with you.

oing it alone is fine, but doing it with people? That's how empires are built.

Story Time:

Leila wanted to build a community garden. She asked her neighbours for help. Initially, no one wanted to help... she began to wonder if she should give up on her dream. Suddenly, something began to stir inside her while we was eating her lunch. She began to think about how it would benefit different people in her community and then she realised that she had to build a team of people who also believed in her mission and vision to help get others involved. By the end of spring, 14 families were growing food together.

Mission:

Join a team. Start a group. Or build something with a friend. The magic is in “we.”

Chapter Nine

Competence – Be Good at What You Do

CHAPTER 9

Chapter 9 is all about competence - building the skills that help you do things well. Being competent doesn't mean being perfect. It means practicing with intention, learning step by step, and sticking with it until you're proud of your progress. When you focus on getting better, not just being the best, you grow in confidence and ability.

Tariq's story below is a great example. He had no clue how to design a website at first, but instead of giving up, he committed to watching tutorials for just an hour every weekend. Slowly, he picked up the skills he needed. Three months later, he launched his very own mini blog. That didn't happen by magic, it happened through steady learning and consistent effort.

To grow your own competence, start building a Skill Bank. Learn one new skill each month. It could be anything drawing, coding, cooking, speaking. Watch, practice, repeat. And when you get the hang of it, teach someone else. Sharing what you've learned helps lock in your knowledge and builds a community of learners around you.

Competence means skill. You don't need to be perfect, you just need to practice until you're proud.

Story Time:

Tariq didn't know how to design a website, so he watched videos, attended webinars and seminars and hired a mentor for an hour every weekend. Three months later, he launched his own mini blog.

Build Your Skill Bank:

- Learn one new skill every month
- Watch, practice, and repeat
- Teach someone else what you know

Chapter Ten

Character – Do the Right Thing

CHAPTER 10

Chapter 10 is about character - the values and choices that shape who you truly are. It's not about being perfect or trying to impress others. Real character is what you do when no one's watching. It's doing the right thing simply because it's right, even when it's hard or inconvenient. This quiet strength is one of the most powerful traits you can build.

In the story below Ava showed strong character one ordinary day. She saw someone being bullied and had a choice: walk away or step up. She chose courage and kindness. She stood beside the person and said, “Wanna sit with me?” It was a small moment, but a powerful one. Ava didn’t do it for attention, she did it because it was the right thing. That’s what made her a quiet hero.

Your challenge this week? Do three kind things secretly. Don't tell anyone. Don't post it. Just give. Whether it's a note, a helping hand, or a smile to someone having a tough day, these small acts of kindness build your character.

No spotlight needed, just goodness, from the inside out.

Character is what you do when no one's watching. It's your true superpower.

Story Time:
Ava saw someone getting bullied. She felt scared inside, but also knew that she should say or do something. She could've walked away, but she didn't. She stood beside them, because she knew that she would want someone to help her if it were happening to her. "Wanna sit with me?" she said. She became a quiet hero.

Your Challenge:
Do 3 kind things this week. Secretly. No credit. Just goodness.

Chapter Eleven

Contribution – Make the World Better

CHAPTER 11

Chapter 11 is about contribution - using your time, energy, and heart to make the world a better place. It doesn't take fame, money, or big resources to make an impact. Every time you choose to help, give, or care, you add light to the world. Contribution is about noticing what's needed and stepping in, even in small ways.

Sami's story below shows how one small act can grow into something powerful. He started by collecting a few used books to share with kids who didn't have any. What began as a single shelf of stories turned into a movement, eventually filling 50 homes with books. Sami didn't wait for permission or perfection. He simply asked, "How can I help?" and took action.

Now it's your turn. This week, take on the mission: ask how you can help, choose one cause you care about, and start small. Whether it's picking up litter, writing a kind note, or raising awareness for something important, it all matters. The world doesn't need perfect heroes. It just needs people who care enough to contribute.

The world gets brighter every time you decide to help.

Story Time:

Sami started collecting used books and giving them to kids who didn't have any. At times Sami would get rejected, but that did not stop Sami. One bookshelf turned into 50 homes filled with stories.

Your Mission:

- Ask: “How can I help?”
- Find one cause to care about
- Start small. It matters.

Bonus Chapter Twelve

Positioning – Make the World Take You Seriously

BONUS CHAPTER 12

Chapter 12 is your secret weapon: Positioning. It's the step most people don't learn until they're much older, but you're ready now. Positioning means making sure the world sees your talent, your ideas, and your value. You've done the work. You've grown your skills and your character. Now it's time to show up, stand out, and say: "This is who I am, and here's where I'm going."

So how do you position yourself, even as young as 12-years-old or even 100-years-old. Simple: start putting yourself out there. Ask a mentor to guide you. Build your personal brand, be known for something positive and powerful. Publish your thoughts in a blog, podcast, or zine. Write a mini book, speak at school, or share your art online. These small moves send a big message: You take yourself seriously. And when you do that, others will too.

To help you along the way, build your Positioning Toolkit: keep a notebook of big ideas, find someone you admire to learn from, and choose one place to share your work publicly. Most important of all? A brave heart. When you believe in yourself and let the world see what you're made of, the opportunities will start finding you. You're not just preparing for the future... you're creating it now.

You’ve got skills. You’ve got heart. Now it’s time to show the world who you are and where you’re going.

This is your Secret Move... the one most kids don't learn until they're older.

What Is Positioning?

It’s making sure people see your value. It's how you turn all your effort into opportunity.

Ways to Position Yourself (Even at 12 or even if you are 100-years-old!...):

1. Hire a Mentor – Ask someone older who's doing what you want to do. "Can I learn from you?" That one question can change everything.
2. Build Your Personal Brand – What do people say when they hear your name? the "kind kid who's great at art" or the "science genius with big ideas."
3. Start a Publishing House – Create stories. Make magazines. Start a blog or newsletter.
4. Write a Book – You're doing it now! Or write about your hobby. (Even 10 pages makes you an author.)
5. Launch a Podcast – Interview your family, friends or experts doing cool things. Post it online. Boom you're a host.
6. Speak in Public – Join a speaking club, or ask to talk at school, college, university, work or in your business.

Speaking gives you power. Use your voice!

Your Positioning Toolkit

- A notebook for big ideas
- A mentor or coach
- A public place to share (YouTube, blog, art wall)
- A brave heart

Your Superpower Journal

- What's your biggest dream?
- What did you learn from this book?
- Write a letter to your Future Self.

BE YOUR BRAND

Think About *This*

THINK ABOUT THIS – YOU ARE ALREADY SURROUNDED BY OPPORTUNITY

This surprise chapter flips the switch on how you see your world and yourself. It asks a powerful question: What if everything you need to begin is already around you? You don't have to wait to grow up, move somewhere else, or "get chosen." The opportunity isn't far away. It's right under your feet. But you have to be curious enough to notice it, bold enough to believe it, and brave enough to begin.

Elijah's story below is the perfect reminder. He thought nothing big could happen in his small town, until a mysterious letter made him start looking for treasure. While everyone laughed, he kept searching. And then, with his teacher's encouragement, he realised the treasure wasn't in the ground. It was in his ideas, his voice, and the stories of the people around him. When he created "Treasure Talk," he helped his whole town shine and proved that big things can grow from small places.

Now, it's your turn to see the gold. The Hidden Opportunity Hunt and 7-Day Opportunity Challenge give you simple steps to start spotting what others miss. Ask deep questions, say thank you, solve small problems, and share your voice. You already have tools, talents, and people who believe in you. The truth is: you're not waiting to begin... you've already started. And when you look around with vision instead of comparison, you'll see the world opening up in amazing ways.

What if everything you ever needed to start already existed around you? What if you didn't have to wait to be chosen or be older, richer, taller, or "better"?
What if the door was already open and all you had to do was walk through it?

Welcome to the chapter that flips on the light switch.

Story Time: The Mystery of the Invisible Gold

Once there was a kid named Elijah who lived in a small town where nothing seemed to happen. He wanted to make a big impact, but he believed nothing exciting could start until he moved to a "big city" or became famous.

One day, while walking home, he found an old letter on the ground-half-torn, half-soaked. It said:

“There is treasure under your feet, but only those who choose to see it will find it.”

Elijah became obsessed. He searched in the fields, under stones, and even under his bed. He told everyone, “There's gold here!” People laughed.

Until one day, his teacher said:

“Elijah, what if the treasure isn't gold? What if it's you? Your ideas. Your voice. Your story. Your kindness.”

That night, Elijah stopped digging and started building. He made a YouTube series called “Treasure Talk”, interviewing people from his own town about their stories, lessons, and hopes.

Two years later, his channel had a million views and guess what? Everyone saw the gold now. Not in the ground. In the people. In the possibilities. In him.

THINK ABOUT THIS:
You are standing in a field of opportunity, but you'll only see it if you look with curiosity instead of comparison.

You don't need more stuff. You need more vision.
Let's prove it.

Activity: The "Hidden Opportunity Hunt"

1. Look Around:
2. In your room, in your school, in your college, in your university, in your community, at work, in your family, in your home and within your friendship cycles what's missing or needs improving?
3. Think Differently:
4. What's something people say "just is the way it is" that YOU think could be better?
5. Ask This:
6. "What if I did something about it? What would I need?"
7. List 5 Things You Already Have: Example: A phone, a notebook, a friend who's good at video, a teacher who believes in me, a passion for animals, etc.

Now circle one. That's your start.

Deep Questions That Unlock Your Brain

Ask these in a journal—or talk them out loud. They're simple. But powerful.

- What's something I've always wanted to try but didn't think I could?
- Who do I know that I've never asked for help?
- If I believed the world was rooting for me—what would I do differently?
- What's one problem I see every day that I might be uniquely able to help fix?
- What small action could lead to something big if I just kept going?

Mini Revelation Moment:

Every person you admire once stood where you are now: unsure, invisible, maybe even scared.

But they noticed something.

Then they acted.

Then they became.

Now it's your turn.

You already have a brand.

You already have a voice.

You already have ideas, friends, feelings, and fire.

So think about this:

You are not waiting for the starting line.

You've already started.

Your 7-Day Opportunity Challenge

Each day, pick one of these actions. Keep it light—but keep it going.

Day 1

Opportunity Action: Ask someone a deep question you've never asked.

Day 2

Opportunity Action: Start a list of ideas you could turn into a project.

Day 3

Opportunity Action: Say "thank you" to someone who's helped you grow.

Day 4

Opportunity Action: Notice a problem around you—and write down 3 ways to fix it.

Day 5

Opportunity Action: Teach someone something you know well.

Day 6

Opportunity Action: Share a story about your life—written, recorded, or drawn.

Day 7

Opportunity Action: Write a short note to your future self: "Here's what I'm starting now..."

Final Thought:

Your world isn't small. It's just beginning. And sometimes, the biggest opportunities are quiet, waiting for you to notice them.

So don't just chase success.

Spot the gold. Dig in. Show up.

Because the treasure has always been you.

The End

BE

By Amire Ben Salmi

Your

The Ultimate Guide to Unlocking Your Full Potential

Brand

It's time to learn how to Dream Big without limits! - the question is are you ready to soar to new heights?...

BE YOUR BRAND

AFFIRMATIONS

I AM THE AUTHOR OF MY OWN STORY.

MY IDEAS ARE POWERFUL, AND THE WORLD NEEDS THEM.

I CAN FIGURE THINGS OUT, EVEN WHEN IT'S HARD.

I DON'T HAVE TO BE PERFECT.

I SHOW UP, SPEAK UP AND STAND TALL.

EVERY STEP I TAKE BUILDS MY FUTURE.

I TURN MY DREAMS INTO GOALS AND MY GOALS INTO ACTION.

I AM BECOMING THE PERSON I'M MEANT TO BE.

MISTAKES
DON'T STOP ME,
THEY GROW ME.

I SHINE BRIGHTEST WHEN I'M BEING MYSELF.

MY VOICE MATTERS, AND I USE IT WITH KINDNESS AND CONFIDENCE.

I MAKE A DIFFERENCE BY BEING BRAVE AND KIND.

I BUILD MY BRAND BY BEING REAL, BOLD AND TRUE.

I HAVE WHAT IT TAKES TO SUCCEED AND I'M JUST GETTING STARTED.

I AM A TRAILBLAZER AND THE WORLD BETTER GET READY.

BE YOUR BRAND

Notes

BE YOUR BRAND

The Ultimate Guide to Unlocking Your Full Potential

BE YOUR BRAND

The Ultimate Guide to Unlocking Your Full Potential

BE YOUR BRAND

The Ultimate Guide to Unlocking Your Full Potential

BE YOUR BRAND

The Ultimate Guide to Unlocking Your Full Potential

BE YOUR BRAND

The Ultimate Guide to Unlocking Your Full Potential

BE YOUR BRAND

The Ultimate Guide to Unlocking Your Full Potential

BE YOUR BRAND

The Ultimate Guide to Unlocking Your Full Potential

BE YOUR BRAND

The Ultimate Guide to Unlocking Your Full Potential

BE Your Brand

BE YOUR BRAND

The Ultimate Guide to Unlocking Your Full Potential

BE YOUR BRAND

The Ultimate Guide to Unlocking Your Full Potential

BE YOUR BRAND

The Ultimate Guide to Unlocking Your Full Potential

BE YOUR BRAND

The Ultimate Guide to Unlocking Your Full Potential

BE YOUR BRAND

The Ultimate Guide to Unlocking Your Full Potential

BE YOUR BRAND

The Ultimate Guide to Unlocking Your Full Potential

BE YOUR BRAND

The Ultimate Guide to Unlocking Your Full Potential

BE YOUR BRAND

The Ultimate Guide to Unlocking Your Full Potential

BE YOUR BRAND

The Ultimate Guide to Unlocking Your Full Potential

BE Your Brand

By Amire Ben Salmi

The Ultimate Guide to Unlocking Your Full Potential

It's time to learn how to Dream Big without limits! - the question is are you ready to soar to new heights?...

GLOBAL BLACK IMPACT SUMMIT
CLG
African Energy Chamber
BIF
BLACK IMPACT FOUNDATION
AMIRE BEN SALMI
I AM A LEADER

Black Impact Foundation

BLACK IMPACT FOUNDATION

Making impact together

Vision

Create a cohesive global black community where black people across the globe are empowered to take control and improve the quality of their lives, assert their value, and be protected from exploitation while building their capacity for social economic independence and social responsibility. Embracing everyone who identifies him/herself as black and everyone with an affinity with the black global community.

Mission

The organisation aims to be a solid pillar and catalyst to empower, build, protect, sustain and further develop an inclusive and equal society through entrepreneurship, education, research and legal support to improve the overall development of, character, sense of worth, and a flourishing value system while encouraging social mobility.

For more information about the Black Impact Foundation please visit their website: www.blackimpactfoundation.com

BE YOUR BRAND

Global Black Impact Summit

A Focus on Black Excellence

The 2024 iteration of the Global Black Impact Summit (GBIS) was a landmark event, centered around the theme "Black Excellence: Unleashing the Unexplored Potential for Global Unity." This theme underscored the Black Impact Foundation's unwavering dedication to the promotion of diversity, equity, and empowerment. It served as a driving force behind this significant gathering, uniting participants with a common mission to fortify and cultivate the worldwide Black community.

Who attends?:

Global leaders, Celebrities, International organizations, NGOs & NPOs, Chief diversity officers, Human resources, Global brands, Entrepreneurs/startups, Investors/banks, Government officials, Students, Educators, Young talented people or leaders, Professionals of any specialties of relevance and so many more.

For more information about the Global Black Impact Summit please visit their website: www.globalblackimpact.com

AFRICAN ENERGY CHAMBER

At The Forefront Of The African Energy Industry
We uphold a results-focused business environment for companies operating in Africa's dynamic energy industry. The African Energy Chamber works with indigenous companies throughout the continent in optimizing their reach and networks.
Our partnerships with international dignitaries, executives, and companies allow for relevant servicing to other international entities looking to operate within the continent. The African Energy Chamber brings willing governments and credible businesses together to continuing growth of the African energy sector under international standard business practices.

Africa Is A Powerhouse
With a standard aggregate growth projection expected to continue for the next 15 years, Africa is in the preliminary position of capitalizing on this growth through strategic partnerships and trade.
Reduction in barriers of entry in the energy sectors has ushered in more opportunities for new players to profit from our resource rich continent. In developing the energy sector through initiatives, African nations should focus on developing a natural gas market that will service as the foundation of Africa's energy industry. We focus on establishing a strong domestic trading market in this regard.

For more information about the African Energy Chamber please visit their website: www.energychamber.org

About The Author

ABOUT *The* AUTHOR

MEET THE MIND
BEHIND THE MISSION

HTTPS://LINKTR.EE/AMIREBENSALMI

Purpose: To put a smile on the faces of 1 Mission peoples faces starting with you through the teaching of affirmation

Website: https://linktr.ee/AmireBenSalmi

Guest speaker at the Global Black Impact Summit founded by the legendary Clarence Seedorf Chairman, Black Impact Foundation: https://globalblackimpact.com/speakers-2023/

Amire was the youngest to become an author in the Ben Salmi family when he published his first book at 3 and a half years old.

I am proud to contribute alongside my four siblings at the UN SOTF Youth Consultations: https://www.google.co.uk/imgres?imgurl=https%3A%2F%2Fpbs.twimg.com%2Fmedia%2FGBkDkDxXcAA1vxf.jpg&tbnid=V4HhRVYHclmTmM&vet=1&imgrefurl=https%3A%2F%2Ftwitter.com%2Fswissyouthreps%2Fstatus%2F1736423620258218476&docid=eoREzuekyA8Q4M&w=1080&h=1080&hl=en-gb&source=sh%2Fx%2Fim%2Fm4%2F3

Guest speaker alongside his big brother Paolo for an international gathering organised by The Optimisation Hub: https://www.linkedin.com/posts/the-optimisation-hub_nigeria-nigeria-educatedladership-activity-7124013621767995392-gGKT?utm_source=share&utm_medium=member_ios

Amire Ben Salmi also known as Mr. Intelligent is an 12-year-old award-winning author of over 13 books including a book series called: Because I AM Intelligent: Because I AM Intelligent - 365 Affirmations to Brighten Up Your Day, Because I AM Intelligent – Easy As P.I.E Affirmations and Because I AM Intelligent – I Become What I Affirm. 12-year-old Amire is the founder of I AM Publishing House. Amire is the youngest of the Ben Salmi siblings who are as follows: 25-year-old Lashai Ben Salmi, 20-year-old Tray-Sean Ben Salmi, 17-year-old Yasmine Ben Salmi and 16-year-old Paolo Ben Salmi.

ABOUT *The* AUTHOR

MEET THE MIND
BEHIND THE MISSION

HTTPS://LINKTR.EE/AMIREBENSALMI

Amire is proud to be the youngest-ever honorary STEM Ambassador in history for Brunel University London (B.U.L). B.U.L has given the homeschooled families the opportunity to participate in masterclasses for the first time in history thanks to Lesley Warren.

Amire and his family held their 2 Day signature family workshop called Dreaming Big Together - Mamas Secret Recipe at The Hub Chelsea FC and Virgin Money.

Amire and his family have planted their very own fruit forest called the Ben Salmi Forest, which is located in Tanzania. Click on the link below to plant a tree in their forest:
https://forestnation.com/net/forests/bensalmifamilyforest/

BEN SALMI FAMILY MANTRA
"BEN SALMI TEAMWORK MAKES THE DREAMWORK
We believe that there is no such thing as failure, only feedback.
We also believe that the journey of one thousand miles begins with a single step in the right direction

FAMILY ANTHEM

If you want to be somebody,
If you want to go somewhere,
You better wake up and PAY ATTENTION

I'm ready to be somebody,
I'm ready to go somewhere,
I'm ready to wake up and PAY ATTENTION!

The question is ARE YOU?

1 FAMILY, 6 DREAMS, 1 VISION

Being With The Ben Salmis

DREAMING
BIG PUBLISHING
TOGETHER

Master *Publishing*

What Will **Your Legacy** Be In **50 Years?**

Own Your **Publishing** House **Own** Your **Message**

What Our Clients Say

"Sabrina has an **incredible knowledge of publishing and we were so grateful to have her** support us with **setting up our new publishing house, Have It All Publishing,** as well as our most recent book-

Regan Hillyer

BE YOUR BRAND

Let's Stay Connected

Lets STAY CONNECTED

HTTPS://LINKTR.EE/AMIREBENSALMI

Amire Ben Salmi

@AuthorAmireBenSalmi

info@dreamingbigtogether.com

"DREAMS REALLY DO COME TRUE WHEN WE BELIEVE!..

BE

By Amire Ben Salmi

Your

The Ultimate Guide to Unlocking Your Full Potential

Brand

It's time to learn how to Dream Big without limits! - the question is are you ready to soar to new heights?...